Dear Parent:
Your child's love of reading starts here!

Every child learns to read in a different way and at his or her own speed. Some go back and forth between reading levels and read favorite books again and again. Others read through each level in order. You can help your young reader improve and become more confident by encouraging his or her own interests and abilities. From books your child reads with you to the first books he or she reads alone, there are I Can Read Books for every stage of reading:

SHARED READING
Basic language, word repetition, and whimsical illustrations, ideal for sharing with your emergent reader

BEGINNING READING
Short sentences, familiar words, and simple concepts for children eager to read on their own

READING WITH HELP
Engaging stories, longer sentences, and language play for developing readers

READING ALONE
Complex plots, challenging vocabulary, and high-interest topics for the independent reader

ADVANCED READING
Short paragraphs, chapters, and exciting themes for the perfect bridge to chapter books

I Can Read Books have introduced children to the joy of reading since 1957. Featuring award-winning authors and illustrators and a fabulous cast of beloved characters, I Can Read Books set the standard for beginning readers.

A lifetime of discovery begins with the magical words "I Can Read!"

Visit www.icanread.com for information
on enriching your child's reading experience.

ISBN 978-0-06-240425-1 (trade bdg.) — ISBN 978-0-06-240426-8 (pbk.)

20 LSCC 20 19 18 17 16 15 14   ❖   First Edition

Pete the Cat

SNOW DAZE

by James Dean

HARPER
An Imprint of HarperCollinsPublishers

Pete the Cat wakes up
and gets ready for school.
He has show-and-tell today.

"There is no school today,"
says Pete's mom.

"It's a snow day."

"Hooray!" yells Pete.

"Let's go sledding!" says Pete.

"Great idea,"

says his brother, Bob.

Pete puts on his hat,
boots, and mittens.
"I'm ready to go!" he says.

On the way,

Pete makes snowballs.

He throws one at Bob.

Bob throws one back.

Pete makes a snow cat.
"Snow days are way more fun
than school days," he says.

"Sledding hill, here we
come!" says Pete.
He can't wait to get there.

Pete waves to Callie.
"Come sledding with us,"
he says.

The hill is big.

Trey and Emma look small
at the top.

Crunch, crunch goes the snow
as Pete, Bob, and Callie
go up, up, up.

"Whee!" they yell as they go
down, down, down.

"I love snow days!"
says Pete.

On the way home, Pete and
Bob stop at Trey's house.
The hot chocolate is yummy.

"What a fun day!" says Pete.
"Tomorrow at school,
I'll tell my class all about it."

Pete wakes up to more snow.

It's not a school day.

It's another snow day!

Pete makes a snow fort.

He throws
snowballs.

He makes
a snow dog.

Then he has fun sledding.
He can't wait to tell
his teacher about it.

But the next day
is a snow day, too.

There's too
much snow!

Pete and Bob can barely even
open the front door.
"Before you go sledding,
please shovel the walk,"
says Mom.

But shoveling is hard work.
When Pete is done,
he's too tired to go sledding.

Pete misses his teacher.
He misses the other cats
in his class.

Pete can't wait to go back
to school tomorrow.

But when Pete wakes up,
it's snowing.
"Oh no!" he says.
"Not another snow day!"

Pete wants to go to school.
So Pete plows the streets
all by himself.

The other cats rush outside.

They help clear the snow.

Everyone wants to go to school.

The streets are clear and safe.

The bus can drive.

School is open!

All the kids are excited
to see their teacher.
He has a snow day
show-and-tell.

When it's Pete's turn,
he tells everyone about
the fun he had in the snow.

"I love snow days,"
says Pete.
"But I love school best!"